Things I wish I knew at 16
The essential guide to establishing your teenage self

James Grace

Table of content

Chapter 1

You don't have to be a people pleaser.

There's nothing fundamentally wrong about being polite or friendly to someone else. In fact, it's a really useful attribute. But it may also be something we do to avoid disappointing others or put pressure on ourselves to live up to an ideal image. A lot of people-pleasers actively choose to behave this way because they are terrified of offending others. It is a terrific method to avoid confrontation, but in the long term it will leave you feeling depleted and dissatisfied. It's hard to be true to yourself when you're continuously adjusting your behavior and words depending on what you believe other people want.

It becomes simple to spend the bulk of your efforts on satisfying other people rather

than concentrating on supplying yourself with happiness. As a consequence, this sort of conduct ultimately generates low self-esteem, feeling that there are too many demands on you, and the development of inadequate coping abilities.
Here are some recommendations that can help you quit being a people-pleaser, embrace yourself, and become a lot happier human being.

Step 1:

Be genuine to yourself instead of trying to fit in.
The most essential thing to remember about your actions is to be loyal to yourself. Avoid doing anything simply because it'll make you appear good in someone else's eyes, and stick to what you know is correct for you. If you've been put in a position and asked to do something that you don't feel comfortable with, don't be scared to hold your ground. It demonstrates that you are

powerful enough to make your own judgments.

You may quit being a people-pleaser, but not by altering who you are. Instead, be honest to yourself, and others will appreciate you for it.

Step 2:

Learn to say "NO"

Yes, this is a hard one

Sometimes people-pleasing may become such a deeply entrenched habit that you have to persuade yourself that it is alright to say "no". It's alright to put yourself first and say "no" if someone asks you for something you don't want to do, or if they ask you for something absurd or unattainable. You also need to quit answering "yes" when you are not getting anything out of the work at hand and are simply doing it because the other person is asking you for aid.

The most crucial aspect of this is reminding yourself that saying "no" when you mean it isn't being selfish, it's taking care of yourself.

Step 3:

Set healthy limits.

People-pleasers are frequently ignorant of the limits they need to create in their life. But you may start by recognizing what you are doing.

This could seem tough at first, but it is crucial that you start observing what is occurring and identify things that need to change. Make a list of the things you are doing that make you feel sad or used, such as fetching coffee for a colleague, and rank them in order of significance with the most critical ones on top.

This simple method might help you to stay true to yourself without feeling the need to impress everyone. Boundaries provide you the freedom to say "no" when another person requests for assistance or takes advantage of your time. Remember, you are not selfish—you are simply secure enough in who you are that you know it's alright not to comply with someone's wishes all the time.

Step 4:

Stop making excuses.

The instant you stop creating excuses, you'll have more time and energy to accomplish what you actually want to do. You'll feel more in control of your life and less of a victim to other people's expectations.

If you offer an excuse every time someone asks you to do anything for them — as in "Sorry, I'm afraid I can't do it, because..." — then it may lead to a lack of work-life balance and leave little time for personal hobbies. (In other words: You'll become burnt out.) It also means that people will start taking advantage of your good nature — and there's nothing more annoying than being exploited and taken advantage of!

Next time someone asks for a favor or asks you to do anything that takes up your time or energy, simply refuse their request without an apology. If they inquire why, tell them that you are in the midst of working on your own personal growth and would prefer to concentrate on that right now, or something similar. It's alright if they don't understand at first, since chances are they will ultimately comprehend why it's vital for you.

Step5:

Listen to your inner voice.

Life is a journey, and on that road you will encounter many individuals who will desire things from you. You may find yourself being someone else's doormat in order to get them to like you. The issue with this is that it will limit you from being able to be happy and make your own choices.

If you want to quit being a people-pleaser, then start listening to what your inner voice is saying to you. This voice may be telling you that some individuals are poisonous and that they aren't worth it.

Meditation can also be used to strengthen your inner voice so that it is not drowned out by the loud voices of those around you. Meditation can help you become more aware of your true desires and how to achieve them more easily on your own. Spend some time alone.

Spending time alone is vital for your mental and physical wellness. Many individuals are terrified of being alone since they think that they may grow lonely, bored, or worried.

All these are incorrect assumptions that emerge from current civilization with its hyper-connected globe. When you are alone, there is no one to satisfy except yourself. You don't need to worry about what other people will think of you when you're enjoying isolation.

Spending time alone may help us understand our own ideas, emotions, and needs better. It may also assist us discover what makes us happy or miserable. Being able to know oneself better may be really useful in many ways.

There are several advantages of spending time alone that make it worth trying out, even if only for a short while each week.\s*

Remember that you can't satisfy everyone.

It is a terrible pill to take, but you have to recognize that you can't keep everyone happy. The basic reality is that you can't satisfy everyone all the time since people's requirements are diverse from person to person. Acting in a specific manner to satisfy one person may hurt or offend someone else.

Instead, strive to behave truthfully and those who like the real you will respect you for who you are.\s*

Learn to be aggressive and stick up for yourself.

There are instances when individuals don't realize that they're troubling you. They could be your friends or relatives, and they might have excellent intentions. But if you've had enough, it's time to take a stance.

You may inform them in any number of ways, whether it's clearly and up-front, or more discreetly, for instance by changing the topic. You can also convey your message through body language. It takes a little work, but being aggressive is a crucial life skill for everyone to acquire.

It's crucial not to allow people to influence how you live your life and how you feel about yourself. Being assertive can help you create limits and make sure that those boundaries are respected by everyone around you.

Step 6:

Ask others for aid.

Asking for assistance is a key step in overcoming people-pleasing. It's not going to be straightforward, particularly if you are accustomed to being the go-to person in your network of friends and family. But it is healthy for you and for those around you to start asking people for assistance, rather than attempting to handle everything alone. Start by asking a person close to you, such as your spouse or closest friend, for input on how frequently they observe you doing too much. They may also be able to provide a useful perspective on how they feel when others say no to them, allowing you to understand that it is not as frightening as you first imagined.

Step 7:

Accept yourself.

When you give in to people-pleasing, you lose touch with who you are. You start to believe that your worth may be assessed by what other people think of you. But this is not the case. Accepting your imperfections is challenging.

The more time and energy you spend attempting to impress someone else, the less time and energy you have for yourself or the things that mean most to you. The only way out of this scenario is to stop thinking about what others think of us and truly embrace ourselves as we are.

It's OK not to be flawless. You're a human, and you're going to make mistakes, but it's good to keep moving ahead as long as you learn from them and are honest with yourself about what you can do better.

Accepting oneself entails recognizing your own skills and shortcomings and using them to your advantage. When you embrace yourself for who you are, everyone else will ultimately follow suit.\s* Be more honest about your emotions.

Being honest is the best policy! In life you will experience rejection at some time, and you should be ready for it. However, if you are honest with them, it will open up new avenues for you.

When interacting with family and friends, honesty is a virtue. It is always preferable to express yourself than to retain bitterness or wrath. When speaking about your sentiments with someone else, it is crucial that they know about your genuine objectives and motives behind what you say. Being upfront about your emotions also helps other people understand you better as well.

Step 8:

Don't linger on your past.

Dwelling on the past can only bring up unpleasant sentiments and emotions. You will undoubtedly feel regretful or maybe even guilty. This is not something you should allow yourself to do.

The greatest approach to start anew is by letting go of the things that are dragging you down and holding you back from becoming your best self. You may even need to break connections with toxic individuals in your life or with those who have been taking advantage of your goodwill for too long now.

If you want to quit becoming a people-pleaser, don't dwell on your previous mistakes. Only focus on the acts you can perform right now that will make you happy.

Step 9:

Make yourself a priority - it's entirely natural

It is crucial to recognize how much may be provided for free before being taken advantage of or feeling animosity towards the folks who take up so much of our time. It's time to quit trying to satisfy everyone.

It is about recognizing what you want out of life, making it your top priority, and then attaining it by not allowing other people's needs to come first all the time.

People-pleasers are generally dissatisfied and worried. They never seem to know when to quit being so accommodating. It might be hard to escape the pattern of pleasing

others, but it's necessary if you want to be happy and healthy.
You should make yourself a priority by putting your needs first, even if that means disappointing someone else who has requested something of you that is tough or seems like more than you can handle.

Step 10:

Make Yourself Happy!
Being a people-pleaser is an unhealthy way of life that may lead to tiredness, tension, and even melancholy.
It is critical to have control over your life and to recognize your own worth.
Pleasing may become a bad habit that is tough to overcome. But with time, patience, and perseverance, anything is possible.
So, if you're feeling anxious or exhausted because of the people you've been working hard for, remember that you, too, deserve happiness. You are not simply meeting the

needs of others. Don't forget about your own needs!

Doing what others want you to do isn't as important as doing what's best for you. It's OK to refuse to join a club that your parents want you to join, or to refuse to participate in some dubious plans your friends have. But be warned: not pleasing others may mean letting people down from time to time, which is perfectly fine.

Chapter 2

You don't need to be good at everything.

No matter how well-rounded you aspire to be, you are never going to be perfect at everything. Stop worrying about what you are awful at or what you are "good enough" at and start concentrating on what you enjoy. Play to your strengths and be confident in what you enjoy and what you have to give.

Of course that is simple to say, but far more tough to really accomplish. Where does one start on the journey to self-acceptance? These three methods truly assist to create balance:

Pick something you enjoy (even if you believe you are bad at it) and take a class.

Who knows, you could become better! If nothing else, you will have had a fresh experience and a little pleasure. This is not intended to be some kind of masochistic

exercise where you remind yourself over and over that you are not good at something.
The idea here is: Who cares if you are not good at this specific talent? Maybe you will find you are not as bad as you thought. Maybe you will be worse than you thought. If that is the case, you will have tried something new and gained a greater appreciation for those who have a skill set different from your own. Here is a practical guide to follow;

Step 1:

Develop a talent you have.
You know that one thing you have loved since grade school that brings you to your happy place? Sharpen those talents, girl! Be it vocal classes, painting class, joining an adult sports team, or even simply (regularly!) playing your musical instrument.

Step 2:

Accept yourself as you.

Acknowledge that you have flaws but also actively acknowledge that you have strengths. Do not neglect your inherent strengths because you are too busy focused on what everyone else is excellent at.

My favorite phrase by Albert Einstein describes this so eloquently,"Everybody is a genius. But if you assess a fish by its ability to climb a tree, it will spend its entire life feeling that it is stupid." Einstein's statements are particularly valid in respect to a career.

Do not think that you are worthless or pitiful if your abilities do not fit neatly into a socially-accepted pre-packaged vocation. If there isn't one, build one! Do not be scared to be who you are, since that is just what the world needs.

With so much pressure to be the greatest, and with such attention on extracurriculars that can help you get into college, it might seem like you have to be a master at every single thing. The reality is that no one is great at everything they try. Trying new things is great, and having a lot of hobbies can be fun, but you should understand that sometimes you might not be the best – and you don't need to be. Being really good at one thing is just as valuable as being OK at a lot of things. Be as good at one thing and get the best from it.

While trying to be good at everything we're distracted from the tasks where we could make our most valuable contribution.

You don't need to do everything and even be great at it. And if you try, you're just holding yourself back. If you need some help just ask yourself these three questions:

What am I skilled at doing?: We all have natural abilities or skills we've developed that can serve our business. Normally these are already in play, but they're not always front and center. Sometimes we feel obligated to manage parts of our business for which we have no special skill.

What do I enjoy doing?:

Other times, we're skilled at a task, but it saps our energy and joy. Yes, work can be draining. But we all have tasks we find intrinsically rewarding. Hold on to that hat and hand off the others.

What can I uniquely contribute?:

If you're skilled at something you find intrinsically rewarding, the only thing left to consider is whether it's useful in the environment. Or put it this way: Will it lead your life to success? If yes, then that hat is a keeper

Chapter 3

Nobody has it all figured out.

We all know those people who seem to have perfect lives, or perfect grades, or a perfect plan for the future. But the truth is, nobody really knows what they're doing and whether it's the right thing because there is no one right way to be. As you get older, it will become more obvious that everyone is just kind of winging it — in school and careers. As long as you're trying your best, you're doing OK. Things are never quite as perfect as they seem. But learning is kind of everything. It helps us to get what we want and to take us to where we want, even showing us how—so we can become who we want. At its best, it's also figuring out the why of something, which is actually the most important and informative part as far as critical thinking and problem-solving goes.

Here is a quick guide that might help you figure things out.

Nearly every project Tremendousness introduces us to some new idea, process, product, or approach that we've got to quickly understand well enough to explain visually. So all of these approaches tend to blend together, depending on the thing we're seeking to understand.

That said, all of these approaches also apply to life in general—whether you're in school or halfway through a career.

Step 1:

Act

Yeah, just start it as long as it's possible. "starting " often feels like the most effort, but tends to be the most valuable. When you do something over and over, your experience can help you get better at it as you internalize it. That's why it's also referred to as experiential learning. This applies to both kids in school and adults working on their health: in all truth people get to understand better when they discover something on their own and put it into practice

Only starting can continue the flow, that desirable but elusive state of high-quality, productive understanding realized as action or output. Starting, in fact, can lead to flow in all the following ways of learning, and all the following ways of learning can, in fact, be considered "doing" in one case or another.

Step 2:

Imaginative drawing
Our discovery sessions often feature live sketching–drawing out ideas as people say them so we can understand things better and figure out the best way to represent them visually. This is a really fun and effective way to learn. That said, most people (including us) have insecurities

about drawing. There are many, many resources for building your drawing skills. A reflection on why drawing matters, and how we might think about it as distinct from painting. Drawing is symbolic communication, not illusion-making. Not How-To, but What-For. So drawing is another example of how learning helps us get to the why and not just the how or what.

Step 3:

Think

The most abstract, least tangible approach is also the one we probably do the most—simply because we can't help it. A proven way to power-up your thinking, though, includes visualization. I'm not talking about drawing, I'm talking about mentally visualizing actions and outcomes.

Never underestimate the power of visualization. It may sound like a self-help mantra, but a growing body of evidence shows that mental imagery can accelerate learning and improve performance of all sorts of skills.

But there's no reason to limit visualization. And visualization is only one thinking technique—of course we can "think" on things in other ways, and even unconsciously. Taking a walk has been proven to boost creativity and encourage divergent thinking.

Step 4:

Talk

Sure, having a conversation with someone who knows what they're talking about can help you learn. Teachers, tutors, trainers, mentors, and leaders all are relied on for passing along knowledge—much of it simply by speaking with or to us. This is core to our discovery sessions. And interpersonal learning is very effective for people who are eager to interact with others and engage in conversation. But what about those who are less outgoing, or who aren't part of a session?

Self-talk has a bad reputation; muttering to ourselves often seems to be a sign of mental distress. It's not cool to do in public. But talking to ourselves is crucial to self-explaining and generally helpful for learning. For one thing, it slows us down — and when we're more deliberate, we typically gain more from an experience.

Yes, talking to yourself (out loud) can help you learn. As that HBR article notes, one study showed that people who explain ideas to themselves learn almost three times more than those who don't. So speak up! And listen too! Whether you're introverted or extroverted, self-talk can help you better think about your thinking.

Step 5:

Read

While there is plenty of debate about "learning styles" (Visual, Auditory, Reading, and Kinesthetic) and whether they're real or not, there is no debate that the act of reading—or watching, hearing, and doing, for that matter—has been helping people learn for ages. We typically do a lot of reading in order to even get to the drawing part of our work.

"Active reading is a planned, deliberate set of strategies to engage with text-based materials with the purpose of increasing your understanding... But active reading also applies to and facilitates the other steps of the learning cycle; it is critical for preparing, capturing, and reviewing, too."

Reading seems to be the easiest and most accessible way to learn about things we can't or haven't yet experienced for ourselves. That said, reading about something complex like piloting a plane is a very different experience from actually flying, so it can only get you so far.

Step 6:

Write

Reading and writing go hand in hand, but writing has greater possibilities. taking notes. Instructions. Narratives. Lists. Even creating mind maps is a highly beneficial, low-impact technique to organize your thoughts by writing and sorting. If you want to increase your memory, plan your company strategy, get more organized, study for an exam, or plan out your future by writing it down, mind maps can also help you explore and grow creatively.

Writing and mind maps in particular assist us in organizing complex knowledge, understanding and memorization, and the ability to connect what at first glance can seem to be unrelated concepts. Writing is often the first step in one of our highly visual projects so that we can identify and confirm the key plot points that will later need to be illustrated.

Step 7:

Watch

Everyone has fond memories of the times when a video or movie was shown in class. Right, it was more like sitting through a tedious lecture than learning. And that's how we liked it. But because of this viewpoint, it also felt less like learning. It's a different story when you watch a video with the intention of learning, as evidenced by the fact that students today use instructional films to learn everything from how to change a tire to the newest dance fad. Surprisingly, 92% of those who watch digital videos are millennials. Thanks to the availability of educational videos, abstract subjects that previously seemed difficult to teach and understand are now more approachable and clear.

The effectiveness of "see and learn" has been demonstrated via tutorial videos on YouTube and lessons on Khan Academy, and researchers have even pinpointed the brain interactions required for observational learning. You don't have to be a millennial to gain from this, though.

Yes, there are many methods to learn or comprehend something new or complex, and just like anything, each approach has advantages and disadvantages. The "styles of learning" concept is thought to have a flaw in that people don't truly learn in these ways (Visual, Auditory, Reading, and Kinesthetic), but rather prefer to communicate in these ways: “You might enjoy something, but be excellent at it or not good at it ... [preferring a specific learning method] teaches you about how you like to communicate. It tells you nothing about the quality of that communication.”

So if you want to develop at or understand anything better, maybe do a bit of everything: Start, Draw, Think, Talk, Read, Write, Watch. Then maybe you can fly.

Finally, you need to persuade yourself that can genuinely accomplish it and desire to be able to sort things out in every aspect of life

The point is that although finding things out is occasionally related to particular areas, nurturing the more general ability to figure things out is something you can accomplish. The more you employ this method, the more likely you'll apply it in the future. So even if it isn't strictly necessary for you to fix your own computer, repair your toilet or learn how stocks work, the attitude will serve you when you're faced with other problems in life.

Chapter 4

It's OK to like things your friends don't

Your friend group doesn't have to dress the same, listen to the same music, and have the same hobbies. In fact, your life will be more interesting if you have friends with varied interests. So don't feel pressure to collect a group of people who are the same as you, and don't feel like you don't fit in because you like different things than your pals do. The beauty of having friends is embracing and learning from differences.

Every human is born with different innate talents based on their genetics. Genetics also inform the different ways in which people enjoy things. Some people may hate puzzles because they are trivial and annoying, other people may enjoy a mildly challenging puzzle that can be solved in a single sitting, while others enjoy problems that keep them busy and innovating for years. These levels of engagement and focus and enjoyment of tasks rely on three fundamental factors. The first is talent; are you good at the thing you enjoy? The second is practice; do you regularly practice the thing you most enjoy? And the third is progress; can you find yourself growing better and more easily and naturally in execution of the thing you most enjoy? If the answer is yes to all three of these questions then these are the types of activities that generate passion and excellence.

For some folks their innate inclinations are custom fitted for coding. Coding is for people who like to solve many small logical puzzles in a single long instruction set. Coding is a very particular skill. It is similar to mathematics with more exceptions, and similar to poetry with more syntax rules. Some humans enjoy the restrictions of code because they simplify logic with hard errors where code cannot be parsed. Fixing the hard errors and finding a result that works is a small pleasure that only a coder can

enjoy, like only a baker can enjoy the process of crafting a perfect loaf of bread. You need to practice the skill and get good at it, and then when your bread or code comes out perfect only you can enjoy it because you appreciate how tricky it is to get it just right.
Here are some key points you really need to note down

Step 1:

You can't wait on the approval of others to make changes in your life.
While it's helpful to value perspectives of those you respect, be it your family, friends, or mentors, we're all on different pages of life. Ultimately, making a positive change or simply doing what you believe is the best thing for you in your current chapter of life must be honored first and foremost.\s* You don't have to explain yourself. If you choose to explain, don't be defensive.

Whatever the decision is, the best way to share your current path with others is to showcase it in the positive light it deserves..
When questioned, don't feel pressured to explain yourself. Your decision doesn't require justification to anyone, nor do you have to have it all figured out (spoiler alert: no one has it all figured out) (spoiler alert: no one has it all figured out). If you do choose to explain yourself, be sure to use an honest offense. Being defensive is the quickest way to say to others you aren't entirely comfortable with the route you're choosing. It's also the quickest way to lose friends and supporters.

Step 2:

Do it for you, not for the aesthetic or potential response.
In this overly connected universe, it's hard not to fall into the trap of broadcasting our every move to the masses, by way of the

social media trap. Do it because you can and you want to but keep it simple.

Step 3:

Walk humbly. Don't carry your choices around like an ego.

The fastest way to turn people off from your chosen lifestyle is to tout it loud and proud, as if it gives you some sort of bragging rights or a one up on anyone else. Maybe you truly believe that your path represents the best or even the only way to live, or that the chance you're taking is one everyone must take to find meaning.

Whatever it is you've chosen, seek to simply live it out the best you can, rather than rub it in the faces of others. You will never win anyone over nor will you best represent yourself by coming off as high or mighty.

Step 4:

Worry not what they think.

Even when walking humbly, there will always be people who think what you are doing makes zero sense and who might even think you're a little crazy, a little off, a little ... something. I've found the following to be true in my own life. And wherever you are on your own journey, I believe it to be true for you too. Those who know you and your heart will understand the journey you are on, or will at least make the effort to understand.

It's not up to you to convince others to change their own way of thinking or being. It is up to you to walk in honesty and compassion and live by example, as you invite others in for a closer look at the way you're choosing to live, and share with them the rewards that come from living a different kind of existence.

Chapter 5

Feelings are temporary visitors.

In other words, how you feel right now won't last forever. Bad, painful, and embarrassing moments will pass, so give yourself space to process those feelings and trust that whatever they are will feel different with the benefit of time and clarity. This doesn't cheapen your feelings or make them any less important — it's just to say that eventually they will go away just like you feel anger and hurt and soon after they are no more -they don't last forever. So have something brighter to look forward to.

Your Brain Perceives and Acts Upon Emotional Stimuli

Even though we think of emotions as internal states, psychologists define emotions as a combination of cognitions, feelings and actions. This means what we think of as "emotions" includes not only how we feel, but also how we process and respond to those feelings.

To understand this, it's helpful to consider the purpose of emotions. In 1872, Charles Darwin first published "The Expression of the Emotions in Man and Animals," which established that emotions serve an important evolutionary purpose. In order for a species to continue, it needs to survive and pass on its genetic information. Emotions like fear serve to protect you from danger so you can survive to pass on your genes. The "fight-or-flight" response that primes your body to defend itself or run away from danger is also an emotional reaction. Emotions like love and lust give you the desire to reproduce.

For these reasons, the brain takes on the function of evaluating a stimulus -- such as a dog that's about to attack or a beautiful woman batting her eyelashes -- and crafting an emotional response to it. The brain thinks in terms of how it can best respond to a situation in order to survive and reproduce, and it uses emotions as the catalyst to convince the rest of your body to act accordingly.

So while you think you have this strong feelings or emotion for a person or thing release also that they are only for a while. They are just visiting and soon after would go away.

Here are some ways to help you get rid of feelings quickly

Don't try to fight it distract yourself rather

Don't stay by yourself be around people rather

Have a mantra and repeat it often when encountering extreme emotions

Always say the alphabet 2-3 times before you talk or act : this would give you some extra seconds to rethink your decision and lead you often in the right direction.

Chapter 6

Not everyone is having sex.

Research has shown that we think people are having more sex than they actually are. Everyone should have sex in their own time, and shouldn't feel pressured or rushed just because other people may or may not be doing. You shouldn't even be doing what everyone is doing because you are unique and have your own pace
Girls between the ages of 15 and 19 account for 11% of births worldwide, according to the World Health Organization. About 16 million girls in this age group become pregnant, and around one million girls under the age of 15 give birth.
Most health experts warn that having sex too young can cause both physical and emotional problems, and they recommend teens wait until they're mature enough to have sex.

The timing will be different for each person. The reasons behind teens taking the plunge too early vary, but the consequences are the same.

There are different reasons why teens lose their virginity,

These reasons May include risk-taking behaviour, thinking they're in love, media and social media influence, pressure from a partner, peer pressure to be cool and belong, and seeking attention.

Don't be pressured into losing your virginity for whatever reason – be it peer pressure, the need for love or the promise of being in a relationship. The right time is when you're ready. It's a personal decision. You must be emotionally mature enough to handle the consequences of becoming sexually active, so it's a good idea to delay it as long as possible most adviciabe when married.

There are risk and consequences attached to having random sex or before getting married some of them are listed below.

1.

Having sex may seem cool, especially when you're young and you want to fit in with your friends, but it comes with risks. These include but not limited to

Damaging your image Sex can affect the way you feel about yourself or how others feel about you. Most people may see you as a player and you lose your natural tendency to truly love a person and really feel loved. It is relevant for both sexes and this reputation can stay with you for a long period of time.

2.

STDs : You can get infected with STDs and have to live with this for the rest of your life, long after you've broken up with your girlfriend or boyfriend. It might stay forever especially if not realised early enough. These include herpes, chlamydia, genital warts (caused by human papillomavirus or HPV), gonorrhoea, syphilis, and HIV.

Pregnancy : This will change your life on every level as you will be responsible for raising a child. It can even lead to you dropping out of school which will affect your future and lossing your dreams.

3.
HEARTBREAK :You're more vulnerable once you've committed to someone who might not be as committed to you. This can lead to heartbreak and depression. It's common for teens to feel pressured into doing things they aren't comfortable with. If you decide to lose your virginity, there will be consequences to your decision. Y ou may regret breaking your virginity with the wrong person – maybe you had expectations they would be your life partner – or you may regret it if you later realise you weren't ready. The best decision is to wait. Till you are ready and fully developed

4.
PROTECTING YOURSELF

Experts agree it's vital you equip yourself with enough knowledge to handle the experience. Before teenagers can even start thinking about having sex and losing their virginity, they should learn how to protect themselves from sexually transmitted diseases and also be aware of all the birth control options open to them.

And on an emotional level, you should be able to trust the person you're becoming sexually active with and ensure you're in a committed relationship. The person you decide to lose your virginity to should be someone whom you love and trust.

This shouldn't be one-sided – the other person should be in love with you. And importantly be married to them.

Your partner should be someone you can talk about difficult topics, such as feelings, other relationships or if the person has had a sexually transmitted infection.

After having looked at these consequences you can decide for yourself which is better for your life and break your way into having a fulfilled teenage life.

www.ingramcontent.com/pod-product-compliance
Lightning Source LLC
LaVergne TN
LVHW020524160826
845677LV00015B/3895

9798847525411